Framlingham Castle

Nicola Stacey

Introduction

Surrounded by parkland and estates, Framlingham Castle was once at the centre of a vast network of power and influence. Its almost perfectly preserved stone walls and mere still look much as they did in the Middle Ages. The parish church and town are also closely linked to the castle's history.

Built by the Bigod family in the 12th century, the castle was home to the earls and dukes of Norfolk for over 400 years. In the 14th century it passed to the Brotherton family, cousins of the king, then to the Mowbrays, created dukes of Norfolk in 1397. The Howard family inherited it in 1483, and spent lavishly on refurbishing it. These families were the supreme magnates in East Anglia – rich, ambitious and influential at home and abroad.

In the 16th century, the castle was the scene of a national drama, when it was briefly owned by Mary Tudor, daughter of Henry VIII. Pursued by the followers of Lady Jane Grey in 1553, Mary fled to Framlingham and gathered her troops. She was at the castle when she received news that she had been proclaimed England's first ruling queen.

In 1635 the castle was sold to a rich lawyer and philanthropist, Sir Robert Hitcham. At his death a year later, he left instructions for the castle buildings to be demolished and a poorhouse built. After years of legal wrangling, the first poor families arrived in the mid-17th century and a new poorhouse building was erected in 1729. Just over a hundred years later, the last poorhouse inmates left, and the building was used as a parish hall.

Above: Mary Tudor, daughter of Henry VIII, was proclaimed England's first ruling queen at Framlingham Castle in 1553

Facing page: Framlingham Castle seen from the west, with the ruins of the western tower in the foreground

Tour

Framlingham Castle is set on a natural spur, dominating one of two high points above the town. Two deep ditches once surrounded the castle. An outer gate straddled the first of the ditches, near what is now the entrance to the car park. The small pond to the right of the path marks the ditch's location today. The tour starts in front of the main gate to the castle and takes visitors into the inner court, through the poorhouse and up on to the wall-walk. Back at ground level, the tour points out traces of former buildings around the inner court.

FOLLOWING THE TOUR:
The numbers beside the headings highlight key points in the tour and correspond with the small numbered plans in the margins.

◼ EXTERIOR

The path from the ticket office follows the original approach to the castle. The meadow to the right is the castle bailey, and the trees beyond it mark the eastern line of the outer ditch. The path leads to the second line of defence: the steep-sided inner ditch, 8m deep. This was not filled with water but was a dry ditch designed to prevent tunnelling under the walls and made breaching them almost impossible. The complete circuit of this inner ditch remains and is reached by a path to the left of the bridge. Looking west, the remains of the castle's large defensive tower and sizeable earthworks are visible, with the castle mere beyond.

The stone curtain wall visible today was built in about 1190, but there was an earlier castle on the site, built probably in about 1100 and surrounded by a wooden palisade. Its exact layout has never been identified despite excavations inside the castle, but traces of stone buildings associated with this earlier castle can be found inside.

The castle walls, about 10.5m high and 2.3m thick, are built of local flint and septaria, a soft brown calcareous material often used in East Anglia, where little suitable building stone exists. Septaria was extensively used at Orford Castle, 12 miles away on the coast. Orford, built in about 1165, shares other features with Framlingham, and its curtain wall with flanking towers, now lost, may have been the forerunner to the curtain wall here. Dover Castle's rectangular mural towers, built in the 1180s, offer another early parallel. Framlingham's 13 strong towers rise 3.8m above the circuit of the walls. They have sandstone quoins at their corners and arrowloops at the top. These imposing defences – the deep ditch, crenellated battlements, towers and arrowloops at low and high level – make for a formidable first impression.

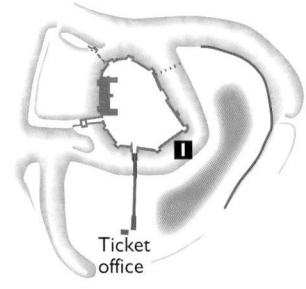

Facing page: One of the Tudor brick chimneys set on top of a Norman tower at Framlingham. Each one is different in design and most are decorative rather than functional

Below: The great tower of nearby Orford Castle, built by Henry II in about 1165
Bottom: The gatehouse and main entrance to Framlingham Castle

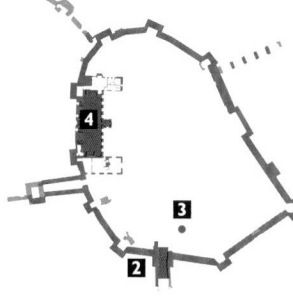

Right: A soldier standing under the gatehouse at Framlingham in the early 20th century. The entrance was rebuilt at the beginning of the 16th century and the coat of arms of the Howard family was carved in stone above it

2 GATEHOUSE

This is the main entrance to the castle, facing the town. It is a Tudor remodelling of the original Norman gateway. The earlier gatehouse was protected by a drawbridge and a portcullis. The original bridge had a longer span than the brick bridge here today, and the remains of its stone piers can be seen from the ditch below, under the arch. At some point in its history a semicircular stone wall was built across the path as an extra line of defence (see the drawing on page 20).

At the beginning of the 16th century the entrance to the castle was rebuilt, probably by Thomas Howard, the second duke of Norfolk. The wooden door has been dated between 1496 and 1528 by tree-ring analysis, and the gatehouse was probably remodelled soon after 1513, when the second duke was honoured for bravery at the battle of Flodden Field. Above the door are the weathered arms of the Howard dukes of Norfolk: two lions rampant, with the heraldry of their ancestors, De Brotherton, Warenne, Mowbray, Segrave and Brews. The Tudor rose is beneath the foot of the lion on the right. The seats on either side of the brick bridge are later additions, probably from the 18th century.

Inside the gate chamber, the Norman joggled stone arch – keyed together with overlapping joints – is similar to that at Orford Castle. The portcullis was suspended behind this arch; the slots for it remain on either side but it has been blocked by the later barrel vault. The gate was always manned and had chambers built over and adjoining it to accommodate the castle porter and other staff. These chambers were rebuilt in brick at the beginning of the 16th century, and a castle inventory from this date describes a bedcover of 'white and green cloth embroidered with white lions and red roses', suggesting that these were well-furnished rooms.

3 WELL

The castle well, 30m deep, is near the gate. Essential in times of siege, fresh water was also important for castle sanitation. The capping of the well is modern, but a 17th-century account describes a more elaborate structure, 'of excellent workmanship, compassed with carved pillars which supported its leaden roof'.

4 GREAT HALL AND POORHOUSE

The only building remaining inside the castle walls today is Framlingham's poorhouse, which provided work and lodging for the town's paupers from the 17th to 19th centuries. The poorhouse was built around the shell of the castle's medieval great hall, which stood on this site from the late 12th until the 17th centuries. Traces of the medieval building are easiest to see inside, although some early stonework remains outside.

At the south end of the poorhouse is a brick building called the Red House, which was built in about 1660 and served as the first poorhouse. It probably replaced the service wing of the medieval hall. (The Red House now contains private accommodation and is not open to the public.)

By 1688, most of the castle's inner buildings had been dismantled. The poorhouse, built in 1729, reused some of the

Above: Two of the five stone heads that survive from the castle's medieval buildings, re-set into the façade of the 18th-century poorhouse. Other buildings inside the castle were decorated with stone and timber coats of arms
Below: The Red House, on the left, was Framlingham's first poorhouse, until the main building in the centre was added in 1729. On the far right are the only surviving remains of the wing of the medieval great hall

medieval castle stone; the five stone heads set into the outside of the building date from the 15th century and may be likenesses of the Mowbray family.

Great hall

Inside the building, it is possible to see features of the medieval hall that once stood here, although distinguishing its various phases is difficult. The earliest hall was built on this site by Roger Bigod II (d.1221), the second earl of Norfolk, in about 1190. About twice the width of the poorhouse building, it would have been open to the roof, and instead of the fireplaces seen today, there would probably have been an open hearth in the centre of the room. At the end of the 13th century, under Roger Bigod IV (d.1306), the fifth earl, the hall seems to have been rebuilt two metres wider. It was covered with lead, and the three lower-level windows in the curtain wall were probably added at this stage. Comfortable private chambers were added to the north; the stone wall seen outside is the east wall of this north range.

The earls and dukes of Norfolk would have dined and entertained their guests in the hall. Its entrance would probably have been at the south end, near what is now the shop. Passing through a screened passage, visitors would then have entered the open space of the hall beyond. It would have been lavishly decorated. An inventory of 1524 describes tapestries with 'diverse beasts and men upon them' hanging on its walls.

There was some refurbishment in the 15th century, under John Mowbray (1415–61), third duke of Norfolk, but nothing of this remains. In the Tudor period, there were further alterations and probably at this time an inner wall was built against the curtain wall to straighten the hall's alignment.

Poorhouse

The rest of this room dates from the poorhouse of 1729. Built with practicality and economy in mind, the poorhouse was arranged over three floors. The ground floor housed the

Daily Life in the Poorhouse

Although poorhouses were set up to provide some 'confinement' of the town's unpalatable poor, they also sought to provide security, comfort and hope for their inmates. Framlingham's poorhouse was overall a good example of its kind. It was administered by a governor, who was answerable to the guardians and overseers of the parish. Advertisements asked for governors 'of good morals and character'.

Work for male inmates was divided between agricultural labour in the summer and cobbling shoes in the winter; the women spun wool. Clothing was basic: a simple dress and apron for women, shirt and breeches for men. Inmates could request additional items – 'a neck handkerchief', 'a pair of stockings', 'a hat' – and occasional luxuries were allowed. It is recorded that 'the girls want gowns to attend church with', and there are also requests for tobacco and snuff. Food was basic but generally sufficient; small quantities of beef, mutton, cheese, potatoes and oatmeal were purchased, alongside beer and tea. Vegetables would have been grown in the castle grounds, and bread was baked in the large poorhouse oven. A note by the Pembroke trustees in 1798 records that pigs, 'both offensive and injurious to health' were being kept in the castle yard, indicating a degree of animal husbandry.

Records were kept of the date of entry, and the departure or death of each inmate, allowing us to follow the lives of certain inmates. Two women (Mary Cada and Elizabeth Woodward) are recorded as escaping, or 'absent without leave', on several occasions. Others are recorded as leaving for domestic service. A young woman called Harriet Pipe arrived at the poorhouse heavily pregnant in October 1810, and gave birth to an illegitimate daughter. She later had two more children, who left the poorhouse, married and found employment. Though Harriet herself was still living on poor relief in Framlingham in 1851, her story illustrates the salvation some might find in the poorhouse system.

> Clothing was basic, but inmates could request a pair of stockings or gowns to attend church with

Top and above: The governors of the poorhouse recorded provisions bought for the inmates in this book, as well as their occasional employment. This detail shows the poignant request for 'white calico for shrouds'

Below: A view of the interior of the castle from 1819 by Henry Davy, which may show some of the inmates of the poorhouse in the inner court

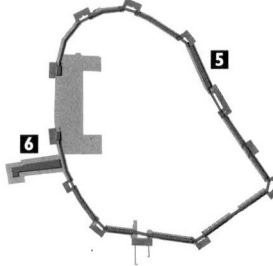

work room, where the inmates were employed spinning or cobbling. According to an inventory of 1806, 22 spinning wheels, 13 shoemakers' lasts and a group of agricultural implements were kept here. The lower windows seem to have been blocked up, and a new window was cut into the curtain wall to light a stairwell to the first floor. The first floor has since been removed but its level is shown by the beam at the north end of the hall. This floor contained various rooms, probably including the 'committee room' where 'three pairs of handcuffs' were kept. The attic above was the dormitory, heated by a fireplace at either end. The hole still visible in the ceiling is a coffin chute, as coffins were not easily brought down the winding stone stairwells.

After the closure of the poorhouse in 1839, the building was adapted for parish use; the poorhouse chambers were removed and galleries inserted. During the 19th and 20th centuries it functioned as a town hall, court house and drill hall.

Further traces of the medieval building can just be made out in the alcove to the right of the wall-walk door, in the castle shop. This was probably the entrance to the first floor of the service wing. The entrance was blocked up in the late 15th or early 16th century when the stone doorway and wall-walk stairs were built. The door on the right up the stairs leads to a small windowless chamber, which was once used to lock up disobedient inmates of the poorhouse.

5 WALL-WALK

The curtain wall was key to the defence of the castle. The wall-walk was the quickest way to move around it and would have been used by sentries in the towers and archers in times of attack. In Tudor times it also gave access to the various chambers built up into the towers. It was wide enough for two people to pass, although with no near-side barriers it

Below: The castle wall-walk: once used by sentries to move around the castle, it now provides wonderful views over the surrounding countryside

THE WEST VIEW OF FRAMLINGHAM-CASTLE, IN THE COUNTY OF SUFFOLK.

would have been risky in high winds. It also, then as now, provided spectacular views over the surrounding countryside – the mere, the woods and park to the north and west and the hills beyond. The parish church can be seen to the south, most clearly through the trees in winter.

6 WESTERN TOWER

The huge stone tower projecting from the curtain wall protected the castle from attack on the west. Contemporary with the stone castle of about 1190, the tower protected the passage through the castle's postern gate below. The high walls of the tower would have forced attackers through a tight entrance, which could be defended from above. The tower also protected soldiers heading out of the castle into the ditch to head off the enemy through a sally port, or escape gate. The fine stone doorway of the sally port is visible from the ditch outside. The tower was originally crenellated along the top, with arrowloops on each side.

The western tower is often called the Prison Tower and it is possible that the deep pit in front of the tower may have served as a dungeon. There was clearly a large prison somewhere in this western part of the castle, as there are references from as early as 1304 to 'the bridge outside the prison gate towards the dovecote'. Among Framlingham's unfortunate prisoners were a thief, caught poaching in the park in 1275, and anti-clerical Lollards in 1428. It seems most likely that the prison chambers were adjacent to the ruined bridge at the north-west corner of the lower court, now almost covered with undergrowth.

By the 16th century, the western tower had been altered to provide a viewing gallery for the earls and dukes and their guests to admire the peaceful garden below. The arrowloops were either blocked up with Tudor brick, or opened out into larger windows. New grand windows were knocked out on each side and new floors were inserted. The joists for these later floors are still visible in the interior wall.

Above: A view of the castle by Samuel and Nathaniel Buck in 1738, seen from the west, with the western tower in the foreground

Below: Prisoners being taken for execution, accompanied by a priest, in a 15th-century illustration. One of the three Lollard captives at Framlingham Castle in 1428, 'John Waddon', priest, was later burned for heresy

Top: Archers at Framlingham could open wooden shutters to fire on the enemy, as in this late 15th-century manuscript illustration of the capture of Ribodane in France
Above: A close-up of the holes in the merlons, which would once have secured the shutters

7 DEFENCES

Unlike many castles of this period, Framlingham is unusual in that it does not seem to have had a central keep, or great tower, so the curtain wall was its final defence. Possibly the prior existence of stone buildings inside the wall removed the need for extra fortified accommodation. The 13 towers divided up the wall into defensible sections. Timber fighting platforms on the tops of the towers allowed soldiers a wide field of fire across the ditch and along the sides of the walls. Steps would have led up from the wall-walk to the tops of the towers.

The most vulnerable sides of the castle were the south and east, where the land is high. The castle's thin arrowloops were concentrated on these sides. Wooden shutters in the crenels (the gaps between the solid merlons) could be flipped up to allow archers to fire out, and then pulled down to protect them from return fire. The holes in the sides of the merlons for the shutters' hinges are still visible along the wall-walk, most clearly between towers 1 and 2.

Latrines were reached through small doorways in the curtain wall and expelled their contents down chutes out into the ditch below. An example can be seen in tower 13. On the east side of the castle, vaulted chambers can be seen in tower 7. Elsewhere, the holes for floor beams can be seen, for example, in the gate-tower (tower 1) and in the corner tower 4.

8 PORTCULLIS

The portcullis slot can be seen above the gate-tower. Portcullises were generally made of a lattice of oak bars covered with iron, with iron spikes at the bottom. It would have been suspended within the gate-tower with strong

ropes, which could have been slashed for quick release, or winched down. The portcullis was not an impossible barrier to penetrate, but gave the castle's defenders valuable time in case of an attack.

The projecting corner tower 4, further along the wall-walk, is five-sided, unlike the others in the circuit, and provides excellent defence of the high ground of the bailey.

9 TUDOR ROOM IN TOWER 6

In the castle's original design, the eastern tower 6 supported a formidable fighting platform. But by the end of the 15th century the vogue for comfort and privacy meant many of the castle's towers were converted into private chambers. The most fashionable building material was now brick, rather than local flint and septaria. Brick was a warmer and more flexible material than stone, and it was expensive, indicating the wealth of its owners. This tower preserves the best remains of the castle in the Tudor period.

The room built here was reached by the stone spiral staircases from the wall-walk on either side of the tower. Its fireplace, replacing one of the tower's merlons, was topped with a brick chimney. A large window looked out on to what was probably by this time a garden in the bailey below, with 'arbours, pleasant walks and trees planted for profit and delight'. With one of the most desirable views in the castle, this room may have been furnished with wall-hangings, carpets, silk cushions, velvet curtains and satin bedcovers, as described in the castle inventory of 1524. Thomas Howard, the second duke of Norfolk, and contemporary of Henry VIII, wrote of his own 'great hanged bed, plaid with cloth of gold, white damask and black velvet and bordered with the letters T.A.' (for Thomas and Agnes, his wife).

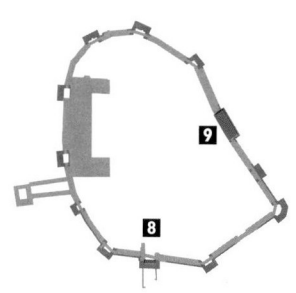

Above: *An illustration of Henry VIII in his chamber, from the 'Psalter of Henry VIII', 1530–47. The Tudor rooms at Framlingham would also have been richly decorated*

VIEW FROM THE TOP OF THE WALL-WALK

1 The lower court

2 The mere

3 Framlingham College

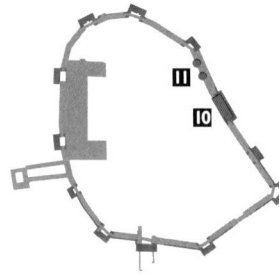

🔟 CHAPEL CHAMBER IN TOWER 6

Beneath the Tudor room, at wall-walk level, are four recesses – two small and two large – built into the outer wall. Clearly not windows, they remain a puzzle. Documents from the 16th and 17th centuries refer to the 'closet over the chapel' and it is possible that this was a vaulted room above the chapel, through which the soldiers passed as they guarded the wall-walk. A 1606 reference to 'iron from the great gunne' stored in the chapel chamber suggests that this room may once have housed a cannon emplacement.

Beyond this tower, to the east of the curtain wall, six stone piers remain from the Tudor bridge. This led out from the chamber block in the inner court, crossing the deep ditch into the garden beyond. The piers still show traces of a stone and brick chequerboard pattern; the superstructure was probably brick. Around the north side of the castle, areas of patched wall and other fireplaces made from thin Tudor brick can be seen.

11 CHIMNEYS

Framlingham's two stone chimneys are the earliest known surviving cylindrical chimneys in England. Dating to about 1150, when the castle's first stone buildings appeared, they served the chamber block below. The stone flues had four round-headed lancet vents, designed to resemble small windows. Their construction is very fine and they were probably once topped by a conical cap. In the early 16th century, the chimneys were extended with Tudor brick.

These two chimneys, and the one in the Tudor room above, served fireplaces beneath them. The others around the

castle walls are mostly decorative, intended to replicate the designs then fashionable at royal palaces of the period, such as Hampton Court. The bricks could be carved, allowing craftsmen to be imaginative, and each chimney has a different pattern – spiralled, zigzagged, herring-boned or interlaced – making a striking feature against the skyline.

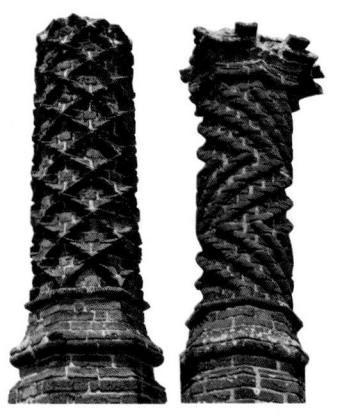

12 FRAMLINGHAM GREAT PARK

Beyond the castle walls, stretching to the north and west, was the castle's great park. It was in existence by at least 1286, and it was maintained until the area was broken up into fields after 1589. It was primarily a deer park, where the earls and dukes of Norfolk, their guests and park servants hunted and caught deer and other game, such as partridges, pheasants and hares.

The park was surrounded by a park pale – a timber fence on the edge of a ditch – which kept the park's deer from escaping. Deer leaps were constructed at points around the pale so that wild deer could jump in and introduce new stock. Sections of Framlingham's park pale are still visible as a bank along the east of the park. The area was partly wooded and partly open glades. There were two lodges inside its perimeter – Great Lodge to the north and Little Lodge nearer the castle. They were used as hunting lodges for the lord and his guests. A parker was responsible for the maintenance and security of the park pale, feeding the deer in winter and dealing with vermin.

Various royal visitors hunted in Framlingham's great park, including 'the French queen' (Mary, sister of Henry VIII and widow of Louis XII of France) in 1517, and courtiers such as Cardinal Wolsey in 1518, as well as local gentry. It also had less

Above: Two of the carved brick Tudor chimneys around the castle walls. Each is different, giving an element of liveliness to the wall-walk
Below: Hunting in the great park was one of the chief entertainments the castle could offer. Records show that alongside the nobles and gentry who came to hunt at Framlingham were various clerics and even prioresses

The Mere, Park and Estate

The mere was an important aesthetic feature in the landscape and also provided geese, ducks and fresh fish for the lord's table. Pigeons were housed in a dovecote on the water

The land surrounding the castle provided it with an income, essential supplies, entertainment and hospitality. The management and exploitation of the landscape also had potent symbolism in the Middle Ages.

Hunting was a courtly leisure activity; the pursuit of game was sometimes likened to the pursuit of a maiden's love. The distribution of venison also cemented relationships between the aristocratic elite. A gift of venison was a means of buying favour and political support, and deer were often exchanged between nobles who had plenty of their own. The right to create a park could only be granted by the king, so parks were a symbol of privilege. Their protected boundaries, exclusivity and organization underlined the lord's control of his land and his subjects.

The mere was an important aesthetic feature in the landscape. Radio-carbon dating of pollen grains in its core indicates that it is an ancient lake, over 3,000 years old, and in the Middle Ages it would have been up to five times the size it is now. The castle walls reflected in the glimmering waters would have made a powerful impression on those looking over from the hill opposite.

The mere was also a valuable resource. It provided geese, ducks and pigeons, which were housed in a dovecote on the water. It also provided fresh fish. Earthwork traces of the medieval fisheries remain along the north edge of the water, visible from the path. Trout, tench, bream and perch would have been hatched here and released into the waters for trapping in nets. Plants growing alongside the mere would have been harvested for food and medicine. Maintenance included the regular digging out of silt brought in from the river Ore.

Four other parks to the west of Framlingham belonged to the earls and dukes of Norfolk: Buchehaye, Oldfrith, Newhaghe and Bradhaye. These provided timber for fuel and construction, charcoal and foraging for pigs.

Above: The castle reflected in the mere
Below: A man fishing, from a French book of hours, c.1407. Fish were bred in special fisheries along the edge of the water

welcome visitors; poaching was a problem, and records show
that local priests were caught. Richard Chamber, parker,
in 1516: 'On holy rood evening I found in the park Sir Johan
Rowse, parish priest of Tanington, with his bow bent and
an arrow in it betting at the herd.' When caught, these
park-breakers could be put in prison or let off with a fine.

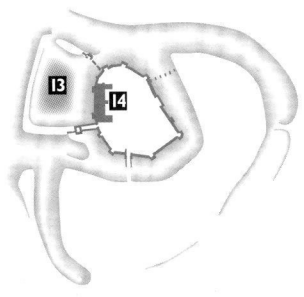

🔢 LOWER COURT

The lower court, immediately west of the castle and
overlooking the mere, was an important early feature of the
castle, built at the same time as the castle's curtain wall.
Defended by two towers and walled on all sides, the lower
court may originally have housed granaries, barns or stables.
Records from the 13th century suggest that its walls were
made of stone and the remains of stone foundations inside
the large earthen banks have also been revealed through a
geophysical survey. The ruined bridge in the north-west corner,
now barely discernible, led out to the castle's great park. It is
likely that hunting parties used this route out of the castle.
The turret staircase of the northern tower is visible inside the
masonry below, probably with a sentry point; next to it are
the remains of a small gateway leading down into the ditch.

By the 16th century, the lower court was probably a
garden, perhaps laid out with herbs, fruit trees and fountains,
from where guests could stroll down to the water's edge.
By the 18th century, there were two fishponds in the centre
of the lower court, still evident in the late 19th century.

🔢 THE LANMAN MUSEUM

Half-way down the stairs from the wall-walk is the Lanman
Museum, housing artefacts from the later history of
Framlingham, collected by a local resident, Harold Lanman
(1893–1979). This is the upper room of the medieval hall's

*Below: The lower court would
have been a private space, similar
to the garden in this 15th-century
manuscript illustration*
*Bottom: The castle's lower court,
seen from the north-west gate
of the castle, leading out to the
great park*

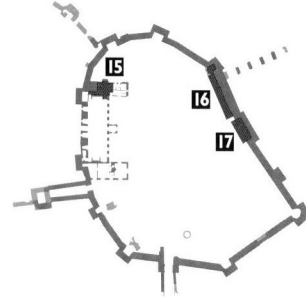

north range and was probably added in the late 13th century. A late 13th-century lancet window is visible opposite in the curtain wall (tower 10) and the jambs of another are at the eastern end of the museum. The stone fireplace dates from the Tudor refurbishment of the castle in the early 16th century. In the 17th century this upper room was referred to as the library, housing 'five old chests'. These possibly contained the castle's valuable archives, kept here until their contents were dispersed in the 18th century.

15 POORHOUSE KITCHEN

The ground floor of the north range has seen several uses. The stone fireplace dates from the early 16th century. By the later part of the 16th century, the castle had fallen into disrepair and the dukes of Norfolk were no longer based at Framlingham, but at their home in Kenninghall, Norfolk. The north range was then rebuilt, perhaps to accommodate the castle bailiff, who oversaw the management of the estate. Tree-ring dating has shown that the timbers of the ceiling were from oak trees felled in the winter of 1585–86. During the 18th century this room became the poorhouse kitchen. A large bread oven was built in the corner, supplying the inmates with one of their staple foods.

16 INNER COURT
Chamber block

On the other side of the inner court are the traces of the earliest, and once the most important, buildings in the castle. What look now like a collection of windows and fireplaces are the remains of the castle's mid-12th-century chamber block, which provided private accommodation for the lord and his family. The building was two storeys high and heated with a large fireplace on each floor. A timber hall may once have stood adjacent to this building to provide appropriate reception spaces, but this was perhaps superseded by the later great hall on the other side of the court.

The chamber block was built by Hugh Bigod, first earl of Norfolk. When the castle's huge stone curtain wall was later added, around 1190, this building was retained and the new wall was built up over the building's wooden rafters, which have left their impression in the masonry. The stone chimney flues (see page 14) were now enclosed within the curtain wall.

This block probably continued to house private rooms throughout the castle's history; tradition holds that Mary Tudor stayed here in 1553. In the late 15th to early 16th centuries, it was refurbished in brick and further windows were cut through the curtain wall. The large central window may have been panelled on either side to provide a pleasant window seat. A window was opened up to create a door that led out to the bridge beyond.

Below: The bread oven, built in the poorhouse kitchen. The timbers above date from 1585–86

Facing page, bottom: Fragment of a late 15th- or early 16th-century mourner, from a tomb in Thetford Priory, where several owners of Framlingham were buried. The carvings in the chapel at Framlingham would have been of similar quality

17 Chapel

Adjacent to the chamber block, and marked by its high east window, are the remains of the castle chapel. The chapel was probably built at the same time as the chamber block, in about 1150, and was also later incorporated into the curtain wall, its width determining the width of the eastern tower built above it. It is still possible to trace the high-pitched roofline of the chapel in the wall, and up close, the two 'skins' of wall set up against each other are just visible. The recesses at the bottom of the curtain wall are the impressions left by the chapel buttresses. At some point, the chapel was enlarged and a second, higher and flatter roofline can be seen above the first. Two stone corbels can just be made out on either side, where the guttering would have led out from the curtain wall.

The chapel was a focal point of castle life, used not only by the nobles of the castle but by their large households. In 1524, it was very richly decorated and furnished, with gold and crimson velvet gospel books, black velvet embroidered altar cloths, silver-gilt candlesticks and gold plate. A tapestry of the story of Christ's Passion hung on the walls and another over the altar, decorated with an image of the crucifixion. When Thomas Howard, the second duke of Norfolk, died, he was laid out in the chapel before his funeral procession to Thetford Priory. A vestry was next to the chapel, housing silk and satin religious vestments.

INNER COURT BUILDINGS

1 Chambers built into the tower

2 12th-century stone window later opened up as a doorway

3 12th-century stone chimneys, extended in Tudor brick

4 Tudor window

5 Eastern window of the chapel

6 Recesses in the wall of the eastern tower

7 Impressions left by the rafters of the mid-12th-century building, encased in the curtain wall. Floor joists can be seen above

A RECONSTRUCTION DRAWING OF THE CASTLE AS IT MIGHT HAVE APPEARED IN THE 1520s, UNDER THE HOWARD DUKES OF NORFOLK

1 Half-moon defence

2 Great hall

3 Great chamber

4 Chamber block

5 Chapel

6 Bridge to outer bailey garden

7 Western tower

8 Lower court garden

9 Prison chambers

10 Dovecote

11 Fishponds

12 Hunting party

13 Little lodge

14 Great lodge

15 Track along boundary of park

Other buildings

Standing today in the empty inner court, there is little sense of crowded and bustling castle life. Timber, stone and – in the Tudor period – brick buildings once lined the walls, but also crossed the castle court to create further enclosed courts. Most of these buildings remained into the 17th century. Zaccheus Leverland, the town's schoolmaster in 1655, recorded: 'Between the hall and the chapel fronting the great gate was a large chamber of stone with several rooms and a cloister under it.' No traces of this central range remain but inventories of the castle rooms suggest that buildings ran east–west across the court at its north end. These may have included reception spaces for the earls and dukes, perhaps the 'great chamber' mentioned in 1524, decorated with counterfeit arras (imitation tapestry) depicting 'the history of Hercules'. The 'cloister' suggests a covered walkway or perhaps an undercroft. The central range may have been an early addition to the castle, although we only have a record of it from the 16th century.

Other rooms in 1524 included a pastry, buttery and wine cellar, which contained a fine collection of gold strainers and goblets. A separate room, the ewry, stored tablecloths, napkins and pitchers. The castle had a wardrobe, armoury and treasury, as well as appropriate staff – a wardrobe-keeper, armour-keeper and treasurer – to look after them. A hundred suits of armour and fifty sheaves of arrows were stored in the armoury. A document of 1303–4 mentions 'the long stable in the castle'. This may have been inside the castle walls, possibly stretching against the long southern wall. In the 16th century there were over 30 horses stabled at Framlingham, including 'an Irish hobby for my Lord's own saddle, colour dun ... a large ambling gelding, colour dapple grey ... a black trotting gelding with white feet and a blaze in the forehead' and 'six cart horses'.

Below: A view of the castle by Samuel Hooper in 1785, showing the remains of a wall running across the inner court

History

The Norman castle at Framlingham dominated East Anglia for over 400 years. Its owners were among the greatest nobles of the Middle Ages, involved in some of the key events of English history, from Magna Carta to the battle of Flodden Field. The castle was also, very briefly, in royal hands. When the Tudor dynasty was challenged in the mid-16th century, all eyes turned to Framlingham, where Mary Tudor made her stand and was proclaimed England's first ruling queen. Though less dramatic, the castle's later history as a poorhouse is fascinating for the detail it provides about the lives of England's poor.

SAXON FRAMLINGHAM

Framlingham's early history is not well recorded. There was a Romano–British settlement nearby, but there is little evidence of an established settlement at Framlingham before the Saxon period. The name Framlingham comes from the Saxon name 'Framela', and means 'homestead or village of the followers of Framela', who was perhaps a Saxon chieftain. In the 1950s, workers laying a pipeline at the castle came across skeletons buried under the pathway south of the main gate. The excavation that followed uncovered a large cemetery in front of the castle, of about 50 men, women and children. The cemetery's date is uncertain, but it is clearly earlier than the entrance to the Norman stone castle. Pottery found near the dead suggests that the cemetery may date from the so-called Middle Saxon period (AD 650–850). As such, it remains tantalizing evidence of pre-Norman settlement at Framlingham. The town ditch, which runs around the east and north of the castle, may relate to this early settlement.

By the time Domesday Book was compiled in 1086, Framlingham was already under Norman control. The Domesday entry reads, 'Aelmer, a thane, held Framlingham. Now Roger Bigot [d] holds.' Until the end of the century, Bigod was a tenant of Hugh d'Avranches, earl of Chester (d.1101), one of the most powerful Norman barons, who held lands around the country. Framlingham at Domesday seems to have been of some significant size, possibly 600 people, and worth £44. Already it had doubled in value since the Conquest, and its population had increased by 50 per cent.

Above: *The head of a figure in chain mail from Thetford Priory, dating from the 13th century. The detail in the sculpture suggests that the figure was of some status, and it could perhaps be Roger Bigod* **Below:** *Thetford Priory in Norfolk, founded by Roger Bigod I between 1103 and 1104*

Facing page: *Thomas Mowbray, created first duke of Norfolk, being appointed earl marshal by Richard II*

THE FIRST NORMAN CASTLE

Roger Bigod I (d.1107), sheriff of Norfolk, was formally granted the manor of Framlingham by Henry I in 1101. The Bigods were Normans, but not originally of noble rank. The name may have its origin in the perjorative 'bigot', and is also perhaps a pun on 'By God'. Over the next two centuries, from their base in the fertile region of East Anglia, the Bigods exploited their service of the Crown and made strategic marriages to move quickly up to the first rank of medieval nobility, acquiring vast lands and power. Between 1103 and 1104, Roger founded the Cluniac priory of Thetford in Norfolk, which was to be the burial place of the earls and dukes of Norfolk until the 16th century.

Evidence for Roger Bigod I's castle at Framlingham remains slim. Certainly Roger would have fortified his new power base, and it is likely that after his death in 1107 his elder son William, followed by his second son Hugh, inherited a timber fortress overlooking Framlingham's mere, and a nascent town to the south.

Above: A seal showing Henry II, who built neighbouring Orford Castle to maintain control of East Anglia in the 12th century
Below: King John, in a hunting scene from a manuscript of the 14th century. He was entertained at Framlingham in 1213 by Roger Bigod II

HENRY II AND HUGH BIGOD

After the death of Henry I in 1135, England became divided by civil war. Although Henry's nephew, Stephen, took the throne, his rule was challenged by Henry's daughter, Matilda. In the war that followed, each side sought allies, creating opportunities for ambitious barons to extend their wealth and power through reward.

Hugh Bigod (d.1177) was particularly ruthless and keen to increase his control of East Anglia. Although he first sided with Stephen, in 1136 he made moves into Norfolk, attempting to take the royal castle at Norwich. In 1140 he rebelled twice against the king, but was created the first earl of Norfolk by Stephen in August of that year. The following year, however, he switched allegiance to Matilda, who confirmed his title as earl. Hugh's dominance over the region increased and eastern Suffolk at this time was described as 'terra Hughonis Bigod' ('the land of Hugh Bigod'). When the archbishop of Canterbury was banished from the country by Stephen, Hugh hosted him and his ecclesiastical court at Framlingham. In 1149 Hugh was described by a contemporary chronicler as an 'inveterate enemy of the king's cause'.

In 1154 Hugh supported the young King Henry II (r.1154–89) to the throne, who confirmed him again as earl of Norfolk. Possibly around this time Hugh constructed the first stone buildings at Framlingham: a chamber block and chapel, which were later incorporated into the eastern curtain wall. The new king was keen to regain control of East Anglia, however, and in 1157 he confiscated all of Hugh's properties in Norfolk and installed royal mercenaries at Framlingham Castle. Although he returned Framlingham to Hugh in 1165, Henry retained the Bigod castle at Walton, and in the 1160s he began work on his own royal East Anglian

stronghold, Orford Castle. In 1173, when Robert, third earl of Leicester, landed at Walton with a force of Flemish mercenaries, Hugh joined him in rebellion. Hugh was defeated and Henry gave instructions for the destruction of the walls of Framlingham Castle. The earl had lost Framlingham for the final time. He died on pilgrimage to Jerusalem between 1176 and 1177.

THE BIGOD EARLS OF NORFOLK AND THE SIEGE OF 1216
Roger Bigod II

In 1189, under King Richard I (r.1189–99), Roger Bigod II (d.1221), gained back his father's title of earl of Norfolk and set about rebuilding the castle at Framlingham. The massive stone curtain walls seen today, strong defences and a commanding position overlooking the mere reflected the status of this powerful magnate. A loyal supporter of Richard, Roger went on to entertain King John (r.1199–1216) at Framlingham in 1213, but later quarrelled with him over his demands for huge military levies. When the barons forced John to accept Magna Carta in 1215 – a document that sought to limit the king's powers and protect the rights of

Below: The Bigod family tree in the 12th and 13th centuries. The owners of Framlingham are highlighted in red

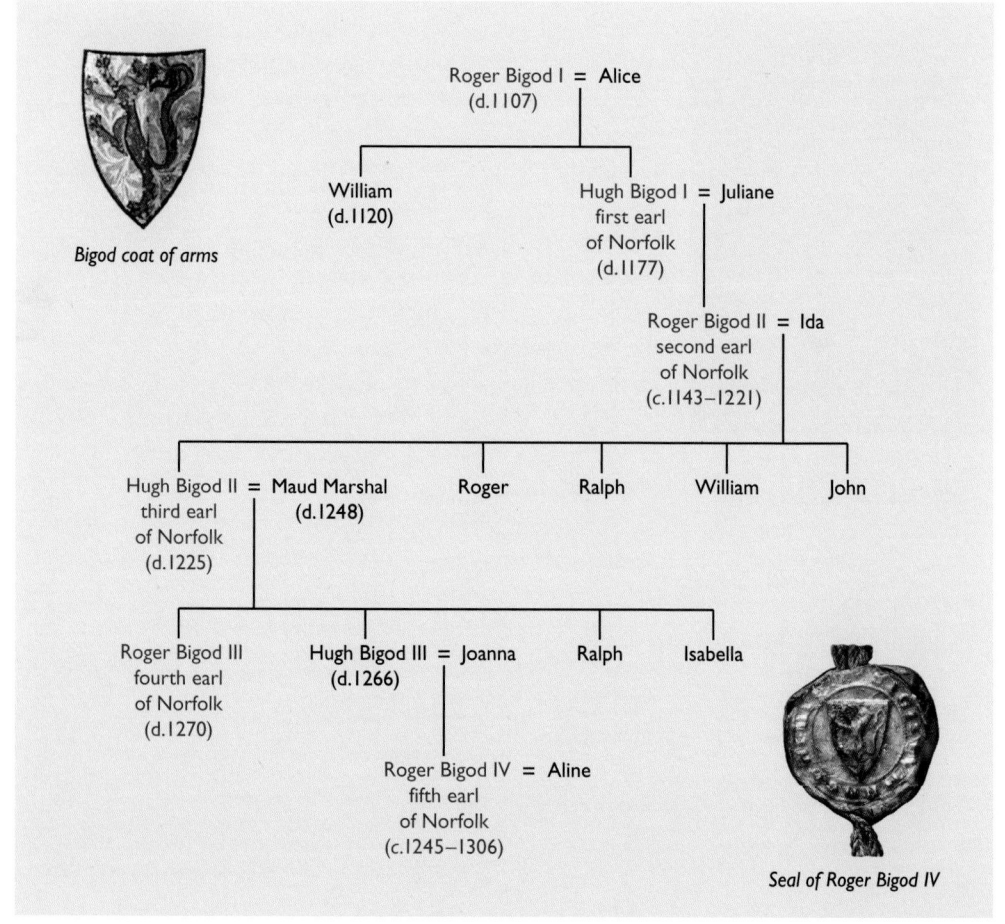

Bigod coat of arms

Roger Bigod I = Alice
(d.1107)

William
(d.1120)

Hugh Bigod I = Juliane
first earl
of Norfolk
(d.1177)

Roger Bigod II = Ida
second earl
of Norfolk
(c.1143–1221)

Hugh Bigod II = Maud Marshal
third earl   (d.1248)
of Norfolk
(d.1225)

Roger   Ralph   William   John

Roger Bigod III
fourth earl
of Norfolk
(d.1270)

Hugh Bigod III = Joanna
(d.1266)

Ralph   Isabella

Roger Bigod IV = Aline
fifth earl
of Norfolk
(c.1245–1306)

Seal of Roger Bigod IV

the barons – the first two among the 25 listed as its enforcers were Roger Bigod II and his son Hugh II (d.1225). John was furious at the humiliation and in 1216 marched to East Anglia with a force of mercenaries and laid siege to the castle. Bigod was away, but Framlingham's garrison had 26 knights, 20 sergeants-at-arms, 7 crossbowmen, 1 chaplain and 3 others, perhaps enough to hold out until Roger returned to command support. Yet the castle surrendered after two days, most likely for political expediency. The loss of the castle was temporary but Roger seems mostly to have retired from public life after this time. He died in 1221, his lands intact, the Bigod powerbase secured and himself a respected figure.

Roger Bigod III

After the unexpected death of Roger's heir, Hugh Bigod II, in 1225, Framlingham passed to Hugh's son, Roger Bigod III, in 1228. The earldom was granted to him by Henry III (r.1216–72) in 1233. Roger was already a wealthy magnate, but in 1248 he received vast lands in south Wales and Ireland on the death of his mother, Maud, the daughter of William Marshal, one of the most powerful men of the early 13th century.

Through his mother, Roger also gained the hereditary title of marshal, one of the most influential royal offices of medieval England. Responsible for keeping order around the king, in peacetime the marshal performed a ceremonial and judicial role, with lucrative rights, such as securing gifts from newly created knights. During wartime, the marshal was responsible for the discipline of the army.

Roger attended Henry III's Court and even hosted the king at Framlingham, but tensions arose over the repayment of debts to the king, as well as a growing criticism of royal government. In 1255 the chronicler Matthew Paris reported an exchange between the two men. When Henry called Roger a traitor, the earl replied, '"You lie. I have never been a traitor, nor shall I ever be. If you are just, how can you harm me?" "I can seize your corn, and thresh it, and sell it," retorted the king. "Do so," said Roger, "and I will send back your threshers without their heads."'

In 1258, Roger was at the head of a rebel group of barons and knights who marched on Westminster Hall, compelling the king to accept major constitutional reforms, known as the Provisions of Oxford. Despite having other property around the country, Roger always retained his strong East Anglian loyalties. He died in 1270 and was buried, like his forefathers, at Thetford Priory.

Roger Bigod IV

His nephew, Roger Bigod IV (1245–1306), inherited the earldom and the Bigod estates, including Framlingham. A contemporary of Edward I (r.1272–1307), and, like his uncle,

'"You lie. I have never been a traitor, nor shall I ever be. If you are just, how can you harm me?" "I can seize your corn, and thresh it, and sell it," retorted the king. "Do so," said Roger, "and I will send back your threshers without their heads."'
Roger Bigod III's exchange with Henry III (pictured above in a 13th-century manuscript) in 1255, as recorded by Matthew Paris, chronicler

serving as earl marshal, he was an important figure in Edward's Welsh wars. The king himself stayed at Framlingham in April 1277, just before the first Welsh campaign, while on a tour to visit the shrine of Our Lady at Walsingham in Norfolk. Their relationship became strained, however, because of Roger's debts, Edward's tax demands and a dispute over the position of marshal. In 1297, Roger refused to fight for Edward in Gascony, France. According to the chronicler Walter of Guisborough, the king warned him, 'By God, O Earl, you shall either go or hang,' to which Roger replied, 'By God, O king, I shall neither go nor hang!' Indeed, he did neither.

Documents from Roger Bigod IV's administration give us a vivid picture of life at Framlingham at the end of the 13th century. Numerous repairs were made to the castle buildings, which were by now at least 70 years old. Carpenters were employed mending the tops of the towers and the 'houses in the castle'; stone repairs were made to the bridge; old walling outside the castle was repaired; new lodgings were built; and the great dairy and the cowshed and the knights' lodgings were re-roofed. The castle would have been in fine condition, and guests entertained in the newly roofed great hall might have enjoyed various entertainments, including the spectacle of a bear, recorded at Framlingham in 1275. Roger was also a great builder in Wales, lavishly embellishing Chepstow Castle and becoming a significant patron of Tintern Abbey. Ultimately, however, the expense of his quarrels with the king, together with his building projects, bankrupted him. He was forced to make Edward his heir and at his death in 1306 relinquished Framlingham, along with his other lands, to the Crown.

'By God, O Earl, you shall either go or hang.' 'By God, O King, I shall neither go nor hang!'
Roger Bigod IV to King Edward I (pictured above in a 13th-century manuscript), refusing to fight for the king in France, 1297

Left: *Chepstow Castle, in south Wales, was owned by Roger Bigod IV, the fifth earl of Norfolk, in the 13th century. Bigod built grand new lodgings at the castle and private apartments in the tower on the bottom left of the picture*

FRAMLINGHAM IN THE 14TH CENTURY

Framlingham passed to Thomas Brotherton, half-brother of Edward II (r.1307–27), in 1312. An unexceptional man, on his death in 1338 his inheritance was divided between his two daughters, Margaret and Alice. In 1362, through marriage to Alice's daughter, Framlingham passed to William Ufford, the earl of Suffolk (1330–82), who led East Anglian resistance to the Peasants' Revolt of 1381. At Ufford's death in 1382, the estate reverted to Margaret, Thomas's elder daughter, who lived at Framlingham for the next 17 years. Margaret Brotherton was a redoubtable woman, revered by the most prominent magnates of the day. She styled herself 'countess marshal', and in 1397 she was created duchess of Norfolk, the first English woman to be a duchess in her own right. It was to Margaret's household that the eight-year-old John of Lancaster, son of King Henry IV (r.1399–1413) and brother of the future King Henry V (r.1413–22), was sent to be educated. Margaret's expenditure was famously lavish and some of her household accounts survive. In one year, between 1385 and 1386, the keeper of the accounts at Framlingham recorded that 70,321 loaves of bread were consumed, over half a ton of Spanish almonds, 40 barrels of red herrings and gallons of red and white wine imported from the St Emilion region of France.

FRAMLINGHAM UNDER THE MOWBRAYS

Margaret Brotherton's grandson and heir, Thomas Mowbray, was created first duke of Norfolk in 1397 by Richard II (r.1377–99), but his dowager grandmother retained her East Anglian lands and estates until her death in 1399. Mowbray himself, exiled for treason to Venice, died only months later, and was never to live at Framlingham. His son, Thomas Mowbray II, briefly inherited the Norfolk estates (although not the title of duke), but was executed for treason in 1405. His estates, including Framlingham, passed to his brother John Mowbray V in 1413, who was restored to the title of second duke of Norfolk in 1425. Mowbray's career was undistinguished, and when he died in 1432, he was buried on the Isle of Axholme in Lincolnshire, near the Mowbray ancestral home, rather than at Thetford Priory, indicating his greater affiliation with the Midlands than with East Anglia.

Above: The seal of Margaret Brotherton, who lived at Framlingham for 17 years and was one of the most prominent women of her day
Below: An antiquarian drawing of 'an ancient window sill' carved in wood, referring to the marriage in 1448 of John Mowbray, fourth duke of Norfolk, and his wife, Elizabeth Talbot

For the next two Mowbray dukes, however, Framlingham was to become the main seat of power. The Paston Letters, a collection of 15th-century letters to and from the Paston family of Norfolk, record the involvement of the Mowbray dukes in East Anglian and national affairs, including the struggle for dominance in East Anglia between the duke of Norfolk and William de la Pole, the first duke of Suffolk (d.1450). John Mowbray VI (d.1461), the third duke, is recorded as summoning an assembly at Framlingham in 1450, to discuss 'our county which standeth right indisposed'. The Pastons, frequently in attendance on the Mowbray dukes at Framlingham, also relate more domestic events, such as the christening of the fourth duke's daughter at Framlingham in 1470. Some refurbishment of the castle probably took place in the mid-15th century. A 17th-century antiquarian account records that 'over the hall gate fairly cut in stone were the arms of Brotherton impaled with Bouchier, quartering Louvain, supported with a lion and an eagle'. These arms commemorate the third duke's marriage to Eleanor Bouchier (d.1474).

In 1461, the 17-year-old John Mowbray VII (d.1476) inherited the dukedom from his father. In some financial difficulty, he sold off some of his estates, including Chepstow, consolidating his lands in East Anglia, Sussex and Surrey. He died unexpectedly at Framlingham in 1476 and was buried, like his father, at Thetford Priory.

Above: King Richard II banishing Henry Bolingbroke, the future Henry IV, and Thomas Mowbray (kneeling), from a 15th-century manuscript illustration. Mowbray died in exile in Venice in 1399

FRAMLINGHAM UNDER THE HOWARDS

The castle passed to the Howard family, descendants of the Mowbrays. Infamous in the 16th century for intrigue under King Henry VIII, the Howards were also brave soldiers and consummate politicians.

John Howard, grandson of Thomas Mowbray I, was made first Howard duke of Norfolk in 1483, by the new king Richard III (r.1483–85). In the brief years of John Howard's tenure, Framlingham underwent substantial repairs and it is possible that some of the Tudor refurbishment around the castle, especially perhaps to the lodgings on the east of the castle, dates from this period.

A loyal supporter of the Yorkist kings during the Wars of the Roses, Howard was over 60 years old in 1485 when he commanded Richard III's troops at the battle of Bosworth, and died in the frontline.

The victory of Henry Tudor at Bosworth ended the Plantaganet royal line. Framlingham was handed to Henry's great ally, John de Vere, earl of Oxford (d.1513), who held the castle along with his other estates in East Anglia. The De Veres evidently stayed at Framlingham, as a later 16th-century inventory of the castle refers to 'Lady of Oxinford's chamber'.

In 1489 Thomas Howard, who had fought alongside his father at Bosworth and had subsequently been imprisoned in the Tower of London, was restored to the title of earl of Surrey, and gradually recovered the Howard estates. Like his father, Surrey was 'early bred to arms' and a courageous soldier. He served as earl marshal at the coronation of Henry VIII (r.1509–47), and became a leading minister at the Tudor court, rivalling even the influence of Cardinal Wolsey. At the age of 70, he led the English forces to a critical victory against King James IV of Scotland at the battle of Flodden Field in 1513. This brought him back the title of duke of Norfolk, which had been forfeited by his family after the battle of Bosworth.

The Funeral of Thomas Howard

In 1524, Thomas Howard, the second Howard duke of Norfolk, died at the age of 80 at Framlingham Castle. On his death he was mourned by many as a national hero, who had secured England from the Scots at the battle of Flodden Field. His magnificent funeral was recorded in detail.

The duke's body lay in state in the castle chapel for four weeks, lit day and night and guarded by 28 retainers. The state chambers of the great court, the chapel and the gatehouse were draped with 440 yards of black cloth. On 22 June, the body was brought out and laid in a chariot of black and gold, pulled by horses in gold trappings and attended by mourners in long black gowns and hoods.

For two days a spectacular procession made its way across the countryside to Thetford Priory, 30 miles away. The procession was led by three groups of friars, knights, squires, gentlemen of his household, treasurer and comptroller, with burning torches in their hands. Then came heralds in liveries of black, carrying the duke's banner, helmet and crest. The chariot itself was next, followed by a line of mourners, the master of the horse, 'then all other lords, knights and gentlemen in black, according to their degree, which were to the number of nine hundred'.

Crowds of villagers came out to greet the 'noble corpse' and join in singing the service. The procession rested overnight at Diss, arriving at Thetford on 23 June. The duke was buried with solemn ritual in a vault in front of the high altar of the priory church, surrounded by 100 wax effigies and lit by 700 burning candles. Alms were dispensed and the funeral was followed by a 'magnificent entertainment' for 1,900 people.

> The state chambers of the great court, the chapel and the gatehouse were draped with 440 yards of black cloth

Above: The Flodden helm, worn by the second duke of Norfolk, now displayed in Framlingham parish church
Below: The funeral of Thomas Howard was a lavish affair. This medieval manuscript shows a similarly grand funeral procession

The Howard Tombs and the Church of St Michael

The tombs of the Howard family are among the most accomplished examples of 16th-century sculpture to have survived in England

As lords of the manor, the earls and dukes of Norfolk held rights over Framlingham's parish church, St Michael's. It was first built in the 12th century, although most of the church's nave is in the Perpendicular style and dates from the 15th century. The church chancel was rebuilt in the 16th century to house the spectacular tombs of the Howard family, which are among the most accomplished examples of 16th-century sculpture to have survived in England, combining the influences of French–Italian Renaissance style with English late Gothic. The fine classical tomb of Sir Robert Hitcham, who founded the poorhouse at Framlingham, is also here.

From the 12th to the early 16th century, most of the earls and dukes of Norfolk were buried at Thetford Priory in Norfolk. In 1540, however, Thetford succumbed to Henry VIII's suppression of the monasteries. As it fell, Thomas Howard, the third duke, tried to negotiate with the king, reminding him that the king's own illegitimate son, Henry Fitzroy, duke of Richmond, was buried at Thetford, alongside the second duke and 'diverse other dukes'. The plea went unheard, however, and Howard began work on a new chancel at Framlingham in which to house his family mausoleum. The duke's disgrace in 1547 (see page 33) put a stop to works. The chancel was only completed in about 1557, by now under the Catholic Queen Mary (r.1553–58).

The tomb of Henry Fitzroy, the king's son (d.1536) and the tomb of the third duke (d.1554) were probably moved from Thetford and completed at Framlingham. The body of the second duke (d.1524) was removed to Lambeth parish church, near his wife, but the Flodden helm, worn by the duke at the battle of Flodden Field, is at Framlingham, displayed above the chancel. The tomb of Henry Howard, 'the poet earl' (d.1547), was erected by his son at Framlingham in 1614.

Top: The church of St Michael, Framlingham
Above: Detail of the tomb of Thomas Howard, third duke of Norfolk
Right: The tomb of Henry Howard, earl of Surrey, erected posthumously in 1614 by his son

Left: Thomas Howard, third duke of Norfolk, who narrowly survived execution by Henry VIII, was imprisoned in the Tower during the reign of Edward VI and only restored to his estates on the accession of Queen Mary in 1553
Below: Henry Howard, earl of Surrey and son of the third duke, was a talented poet and soldier, but was executed on a charge of treason in 1547

He was also granted the honour of augmentation of his family arms – an arrow piercing the mouth of the lion of Scotland. He continued to be active at Court until retiring to Framlingham aged nearly 80. We are told he 'kept a very noble house' and much of the Tudor refurbishment of the castle should probably be dated to his tenure – notably the chimneys, the gatehouse and probably many of the red brick buildings, now lost, inside the castle. Thomas Howard died at Framlingham in 1524.

The next Howard duke of Norfolk, also Thomas Howard (d.1554), was based not at Framlingham but at the newly built ducal residence at Kenninghall in Norfolk, although the castle remained among his East Anglian estates. He was ruthlessly ambitious – a scheming courtier and politician, who promoted and then betrayed two of his nieces at Henry VIII's Court – the king's wives Anne Boleyn and Catherine Howard. By 1547 he had fallen from favour with Henry VIII because of his political machinations and the affront caused by his son, Henry Howard, earl of Surrey, who had angered the king by displaying the arms of Edward the Confessor in his own, and so claiming regal ancestry. A gifted poet and soldier, Henry Howard invented blank verse, as well as the poetic form later used by Shakespeare in his sonnets. On 19 January 1547 Surrey was sent to the block on Tower Hill. His tomb lies in Framlingham church. His father survived, through sheer luck, as the king died the day before his own appointed execution. Instead, his title and lands were surrendered to the Crown, which was now in the hands of the young King Edward VI (r.1547–53).

'Brittle beauty, that nature made so frail,
Whereof the gift is small, and short the season;
Flow'ring today, tomorrow apt to fail,
Tickle treasure, abhorred of reason ...'
from 'The Frailty and Hurtfulness of Beauty' by Henry Howard, above

'When the battle line seemed
fully drawn, sacred Mary rode
out from Framlingham Castle
about 4 o'clock (the day was
a Thursday) to muster and
inspect this most splendid and
loyal army.'
Sir Robert Wingfield, July 1553

FRAMLINGHAM AND QUEEN MARY

Through the disgrace of Thomas Howard, third duke of
Norfolk, Framlingham came into the hands of Mary Tudor,
eldest daughter of Henry VIII and his first wife, Catherine of
Aragon. Mary had been granted most of the Howard estates
in East Anglia in her father's will of 1547 and received
Framlingham in 1552. After the death of her brother
Edward VI in 1553, Framlingham was to play a key role in
the succession crisis.

Although Henry's will named Princess Mary as Edward's
heir, the young king had tried to surrender the Tudor line in
favour of the Protestant Lady Jane Grey. On Edward's death
on 6 July 1553, the duke of Northumberland moved to
secure the succession for his daughter-in-law. As legal heir,
Mary knew her position was dangerous, and on receiving
warning of Northumberland's plans to capture her, she fled
secretly to Cambridgeshire and then to Kenninghall in Norfolk.
From there she moved to Framlingham, the most secure of
her properties, arriving in the evening of 12 July. Installed at
the castle, she raised her standard and rallied her troops.
Thousands of supporters flocked to the castle; not only the
local landed gentry, but the lower classes, 'a great crowd of
country folk'. Defections began to increase in her favour and
further troops arrived with the earls of Sussex and Bath. Five
ships in Ipswich harbour mutinied in her support.

A eulogistic contemporary account, by Sir Robert
Wingfield, describes her hastily assembled troops: 'the
standards were unfurled and the military colours set up;
everyone armed themselves fully as if about to meet the
enemy. The infantry made ready their pikes, the cavalry
brandished lances, the archer bent his bow and girded on
his quiver; the harquebusier filled his weapon with powder…
When the battle line seemed fully drawn, sacred Mary rode
out from Framlingham castle about 4 o'clock (the day was
a Thursday) to muster and inspect this most splendid and
loyal army.'

By 19 July Northumberland had surrendered, and news
reached Mary at Framlingham that the Privy Council in
London had accepted her as queen. Mary moved first to
Ipswich and then to London, where she was crowned queen
on 1 October, amid great celebration.

Mary's debt to the East Anglians who had supported her
was not forgotten; documents survive recording grants for life
to certain gentlemen 'for services at Framlingham in the late
rebellion'. In one of her first acts as queen, Mary released the
elderly Thomas Howard from the Tower and restored his
estates and dukedom, including Framlingham. The duke died,
however, at Kenninghall the following year, and the castle
passed to his grandson, Thomas Howard, who became the
fourth Howard duke.

Above: Queen Mary I, in a portrait
of 1554 by Hans Eworth, holding
the Tudor rose

Facing page: Framlingham from the
west in winter

Above: Catholic priests being hanged and tortured in the stocks, from a book of 1587. During the reign of Elizabeth I, a number of Catholics were imprisoned at Framlingham

Below: Sir Robert Hitcham, benefactor of Framlingham and founder of the poorhouse, the almshouses and a school in the town

'The children not yet borne with gladnesse shall thy pious action into memorye call, and thou shalt live as longe as there shall bee either poore, or any use of charitie.'
Epitaph on the tomb of Sir Robert Hitcham (above)

FRAMLINGHAM IN ELIZABETHAN TIMES

The fourth Howard duke, Thomas Howard, who had, by marriage, added the Arundel estates to the dukedom, was the premier peer in the land during the early years of Queen Elizabeth's reign (r.1558–1603). He was, however, executed in 1572 for his – possibly reluctant – part in a plot to marry Mary, queen of Scots, and overthrow Elizabeth. Framlingham came once more into royal hands. By then the castle was in a bad state of repair. Even in 1547, it had been noted that 'many of the houses of the same castell is in greate decaye and diverse of theme is like to ffalle downe onlesse they be shortly repaired'. In 1589 a further survey was carried out, noting that 'the castle of Framlingham is in great ruyne and decaie in diverse places'. By then the castle would have been occupied by a greatly reduced household, under the administration of a bailiff.

As the country's anti-Catholic laws hardened under Queen Elizabeth, Catholic priests and recusants were imprisoned in Crown properties as 'practisers of sedition' and 'superstition'. In about 1600 Framlingham's prison chambers housed 40 inmates, many of whom were Catholics.

FRAMLINGHAM AND THE POORHOUSE

Framlingham was returned to the Howard family in 1603 by James I (r.1603–25). In 1635, the castle was sold by the heavily indebted Theophilus Howard to a rich lawyer and politician, Sir Robert Hitcham. Hitcham was a Suffolk man, born in the village of Levington, and of humble origins. His father was a yeoman farmer, and it was said that he was 'not born to £200 per annum…nor to £20 nor to £2'. Admitted to Gray's Inn in 1589, Hitcham had a remarkably successful career. He was knighted in 1604 and in 1616 he became senior sergeant-at-law to James I.

He was a controversial figure in Parliament, however, criticized for his flamboyance, and in later years he retired to

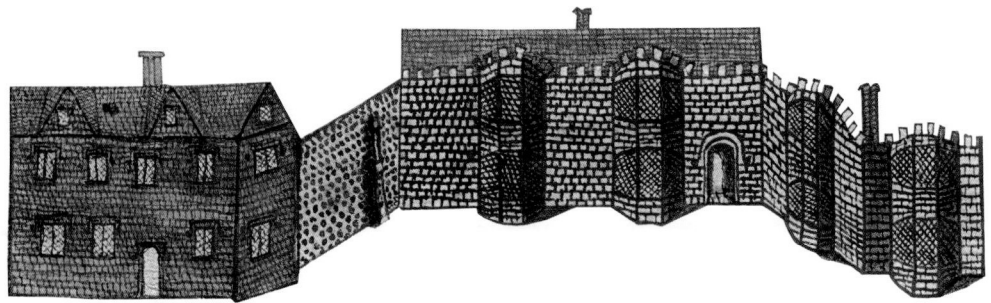

Suffolk, to serve as MP for Orford. He bought Framlingham Castle with its manors and estates for £14,000, a huge sum at the time. Unmarried and with no heirs, at his death in 1636 Sir Robert left the castle and its estates to his old college at Cambridge, Pembroke, on the condition that they followed detailed instructions as to its dispersal.

The key condition of Hitcham's will was that Framlingham and its estates be put in trust for the benefit of the poor of three towns in Suffolk: Framlingham, Debenham and Coggeshall. In particular, he instructed that 'all the castle, saving the stone building, be pulled down' and a poorhouse set up.

The problems of the rural poor had worsened during the 16th century. Under the Poor Law Act of 1601, parishes had to take responsibility for the able-bodied poor by providing them with work and the infirm with poor relief, raised through local taxes. Sir Robert Hitcham was perhaps especially well-placed to understand the benefits of education and opportunity. His will also made provision for almshouses to be built to house 'twelve of the poorest and decrepid people', and a schoolhouse to be built 'to teach 30 or 40 of the poorest and neediest children…to write, read, and cast accounts as the said College shall think fit'. A schoolmaster and a reader (for prayers) were to be appointed and each child was to receive £10 so that they could train as an apprentice.

Top: A schematic drawing of Framlingham's buildings from a manuscript of 1688, showing the Red House on the left and possibly the great chamber crossing the inner court

Below: Sir Robert Hitcham's almshouses, still inhabited today

'Thereby they will be taken from idleness, used to work and an industrious course of life... their poor parents... may better maintain the rest and themselves... and their clothes will last longer than when with their parents whereby they are rent and torn with stealing wood and... at play.'
The Pembroke trustees

Above: The inmates of the poorhouse were kept busy spinning wool, sewing and cobbling, as they are in this 19th-century illustration
Below: A picturesque view of Framlingham Castle and the church by John Constable, c.1815, showing the Tudor bridge leading from the castle out to the bailey

Years of legal wrangling over the will, however, meant that the almshouses were not built until 1654. Soon afterwards, the first new building was erected in the castle, the brick Red House. This was possibly initially intended as a house for the town's schoolmaster, Mr Leverland, but it was soon requisitioned for Framlingham's first poor families. It was, however, impractical as a poorhouse, with 'only three rooms on a floor'. Plague struck Framlingham in 1666, and the castle buildings were used as isolation wards. For the next 30 years, the funds for the poorhouse were mismanaged and it had to be closed entirely. The poor were sent back into the town and for many years a 'Mr John Earl, bailiff', took over the Red House, selling ale.

A further attempt was made to establish a poorhouse for children in 1699. The Pembroke trustees believed that 'thereby they will be taken from idleness, used to work and an industrious course of life'. Instructions were given that 'the poor people in the Red House be forthwith turned out and the house to be repaired and a copper and iron pot to be hanged there to boil with coals'. Yet this enterprise also failed, as there were not 'a sufficient number of children to employ', and in any case a poorhouse 'for older persons' was believed 'more to the satisfaction of the parishioners'.

Finally, in 1729, a new poorhouse was built with parish funds on the site of the medieval castle's hall. This was generally well-run and housed adults and children until 1839, when it closed and the poor were transferred to the larger Union workhouse at nearby Wickham Market.

LATER HISTORY

Despite its relatively peaceful role in the 18th century, the castle again found a military use during the Napoleonic Wars. An account of 1834 notes 'an ancient recess, which during the last war was inclosed with a strong door, and appropriated to the use of the Framlingham Volunteers, as a depot for

ammunition and other warlike stores'. But when the final poorhouse inmates left in 1839, the castle was used for general parish business, and the poorhouse was converted to a parish hall. There was a parish cage (a lock-up) within the castle walls, as well as parish stocks. Victorian Framlingham flourished, with a new railway in the town in 1859, and the red brick Framlingham College, set up to teach Suffolk boys agricultural science, was built on the hill overlooking the mere.

In 1931, a historical pageant was staged at the castle, 'a picturesque survey of the history of Framlingham from earliest times to the 20th century'. This was a lavish affair with a full choir and orchestra, attended by hundreds of local people. It reconstructed different historical occasions in the castle's history, including the foundation of the town of Framlingham, Massachusetts by a descendant of the Suffolk town.

Above: Participants in a medieval pageant staged at Framlingham in 1931

Left: Framlingham College, on the other side of the mere, was founded originally in 1864 to teach agricultural science

During the Second World War, Framlingham was a key nodal point in the country's defence and its open spaces were put to military use. Prefabricated steel Nissen huts as well as a lorry park were set up in the bailey, now Castle Meadow. The pill box just outside the town ditch in the field next to the castle dates from this time. Many town buildings were taken over for military use, and the streets were full of US servicemen from heavy bombardment squadrons. Pilots returning from bombing missions would look out for the familiar outline of Framlingham Castle to direct themselves back to base. The airmen brought some liveliness to the town, and dances were held to entertain the troops, to which local girls were invited. The old control tower on Parham airfield now houses a museum of wartime memorabilia.

Given to the Ministry of Works by Hitcham's old Cambridge college, Pembroke, in 1913, the castle passed to English Heritage in 1984. The mere is owned by Framlingham College and maintained by Suffolk Wildlife Trust.

Above: A First World War victory parade passing the Crown Hotel in Framlingham
Below: Framlingham Castle seen from across the mere, with poppies in bloom